will you be my quarantine?

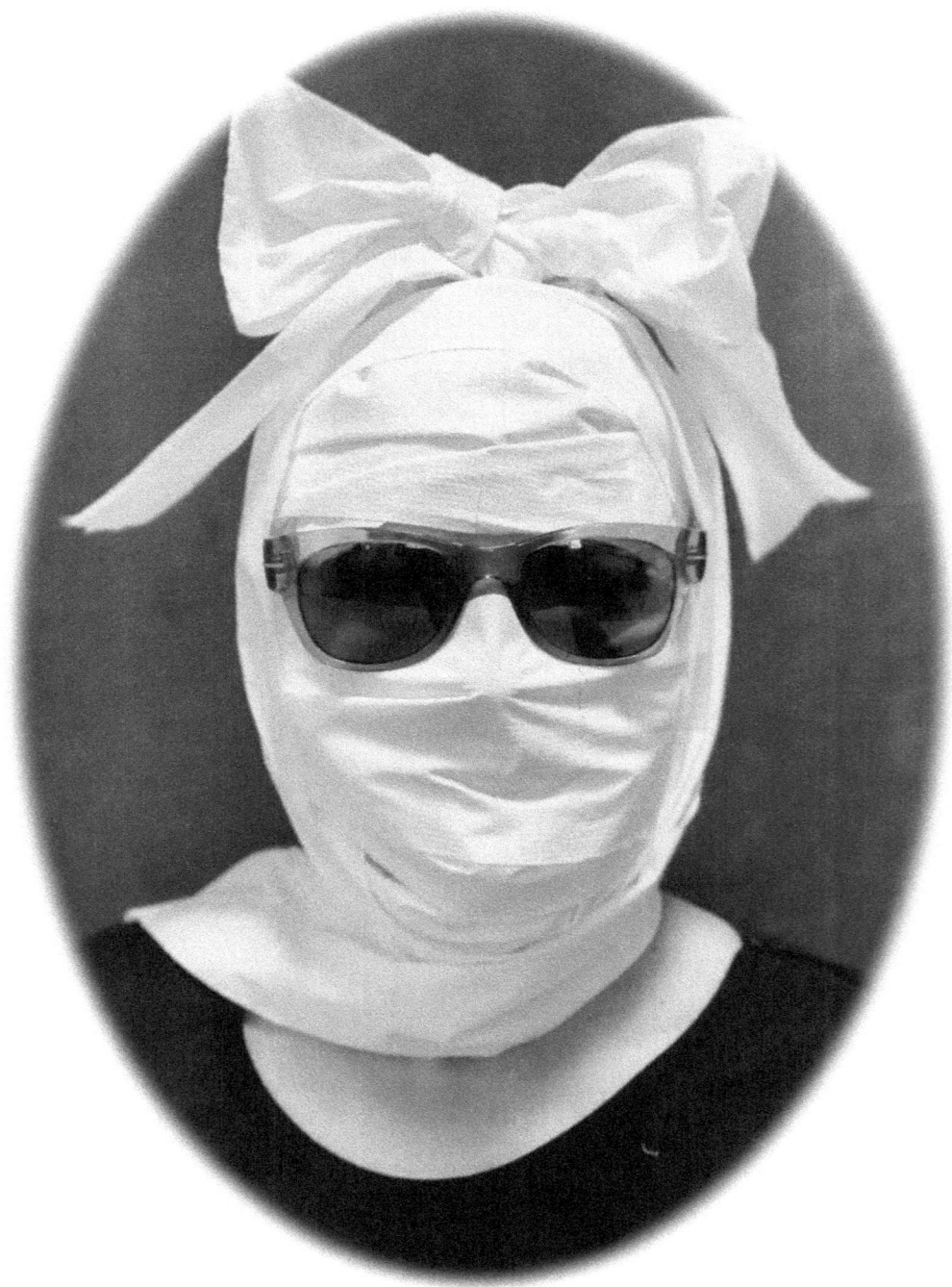

WILL YOU BE MY QUARANTINE?

CREATING INTIMACY IN THE TIME OF CORONAVIRUS:

A LOVE STORY

By

D.R. LEWIS and A.K. WILLIAMS

ILLUSTRATED WITH
PHOTOGRAPHS OF TOILET PAPER,
CREATED BY THE AUTHORS
DURING THEIR QUARANTINE

~ D.R. LEWIS & A.K. WILLIAMS ~

WILL YOU BE MY QUARANTINE?

CREATING INTIMACY IN THE TIME OF CORONAVIRUS: A LOVE STORY

To request permissions, contact the publisher at info@beminequarantine.com.

Paperback: ISBN 978-1-7350814-1-0
eBook: ISBN 978-1-7350814-0-3

Library of Congress Number: 2020909260

Cover art, layout, and photographs by D.R. Lewis & A.K. Williams

Published by Summer Wolf Publishing

www.BeMineQuarantine.com

This book is dedicated

to you.

2 artists

+ a spark

<u>+ a quarantine</u>

= a series of choices

new levels of intimacy

To learn more about the story behind the story,
visit us at
www.beminequarantine.com

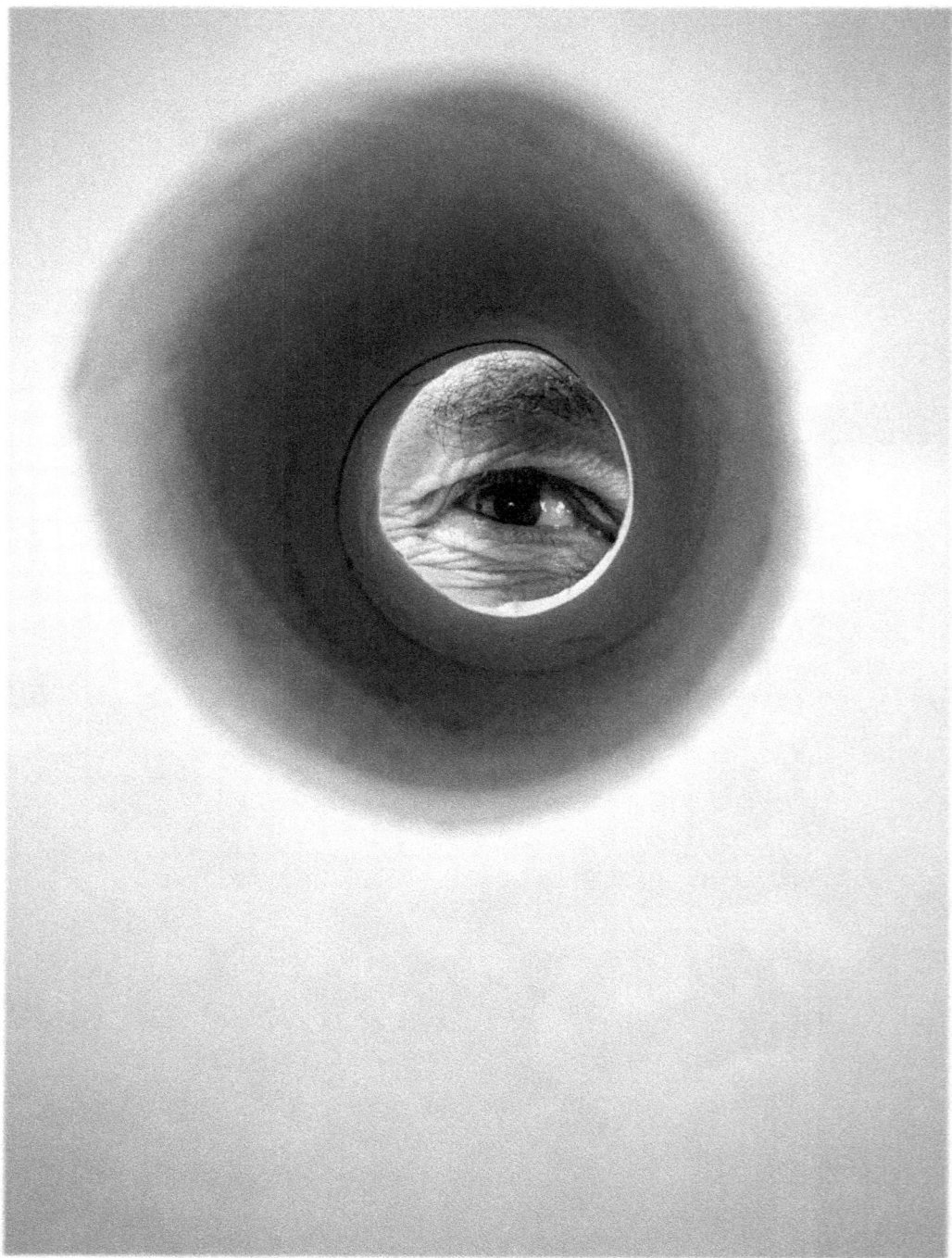

Level I

getting to know you...

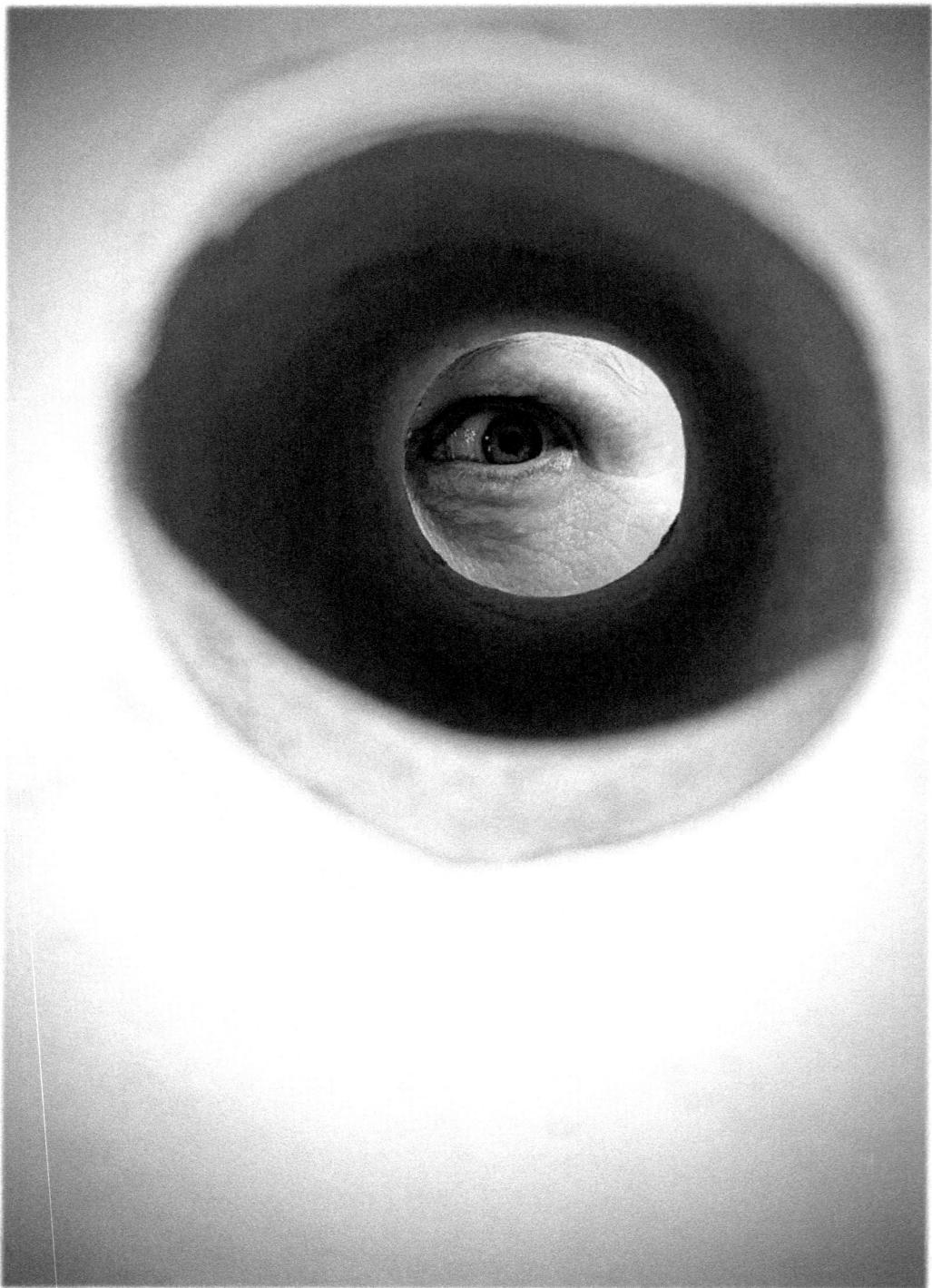

red or green

early bird or night owl

book or movie

canine or feline

fields or woods

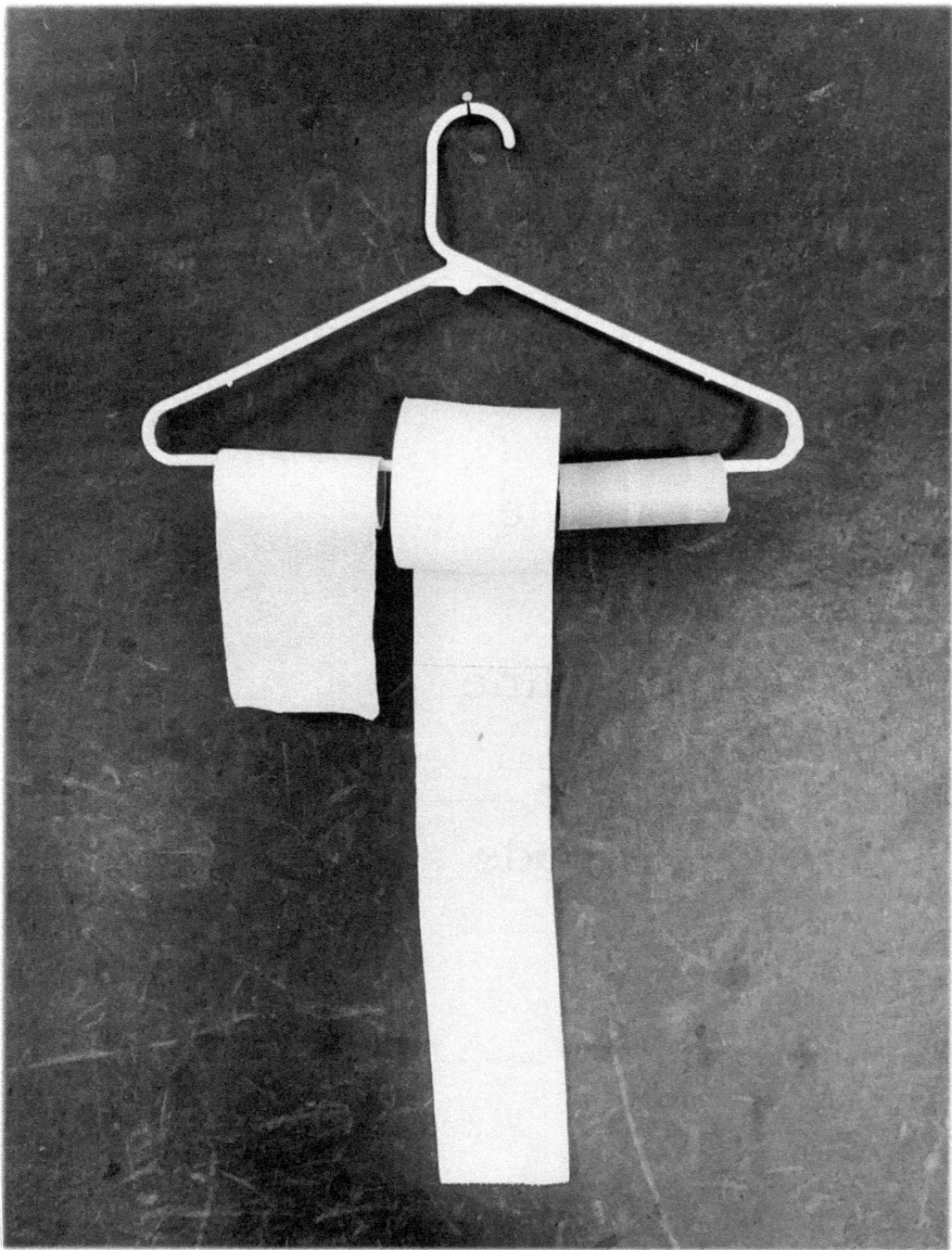

house or high rise

carpet or hardwood

classic or contemporary

on the floor or in the hamper

one pillow or eight

walk or bike

car or truck

drive or ride

talk or music

ask for directions?

train or plane

plan it or wing it

id or passport

window or aisle

carry-on or luggage

europe?

t-shirt or button-down

boots or sneakers

wool or cotton

cut-offs or couture

cowboy hat or baseball cap

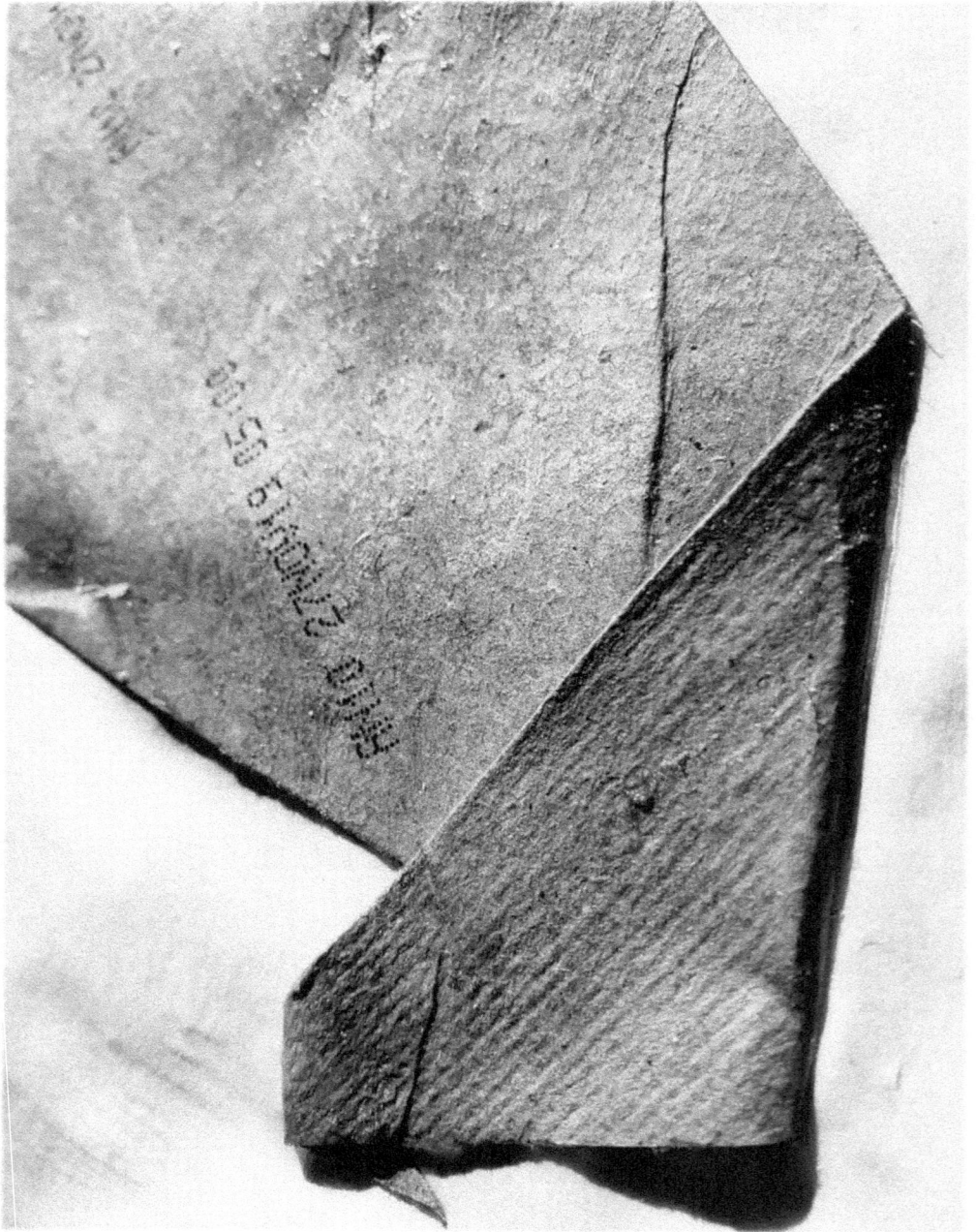

cream or black

salty or sweet

granola or grits

scrambled or fried

bacon or biscuit

fruit?

sandwich or salad

hot or mild

paper or porcelain

surf or turf

street food or gourmet

hot dogs?

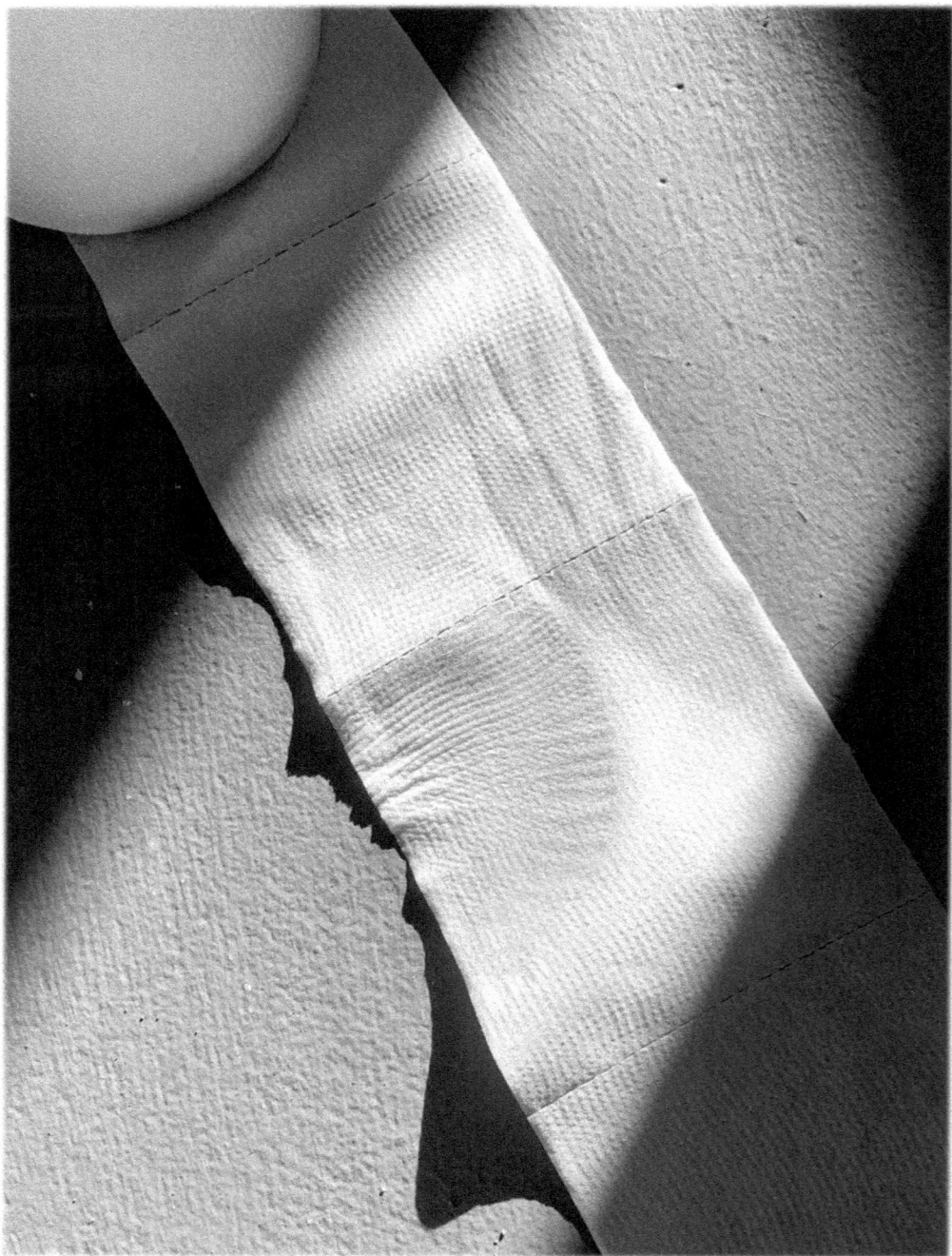

ocean or river

mountains or lakes

humid or arid

wind or rain

nightingale or mockingbird

toilet paper

over the top or off the bottom

wad or fold

a lot or a little

quality or quantity

how much is enough?

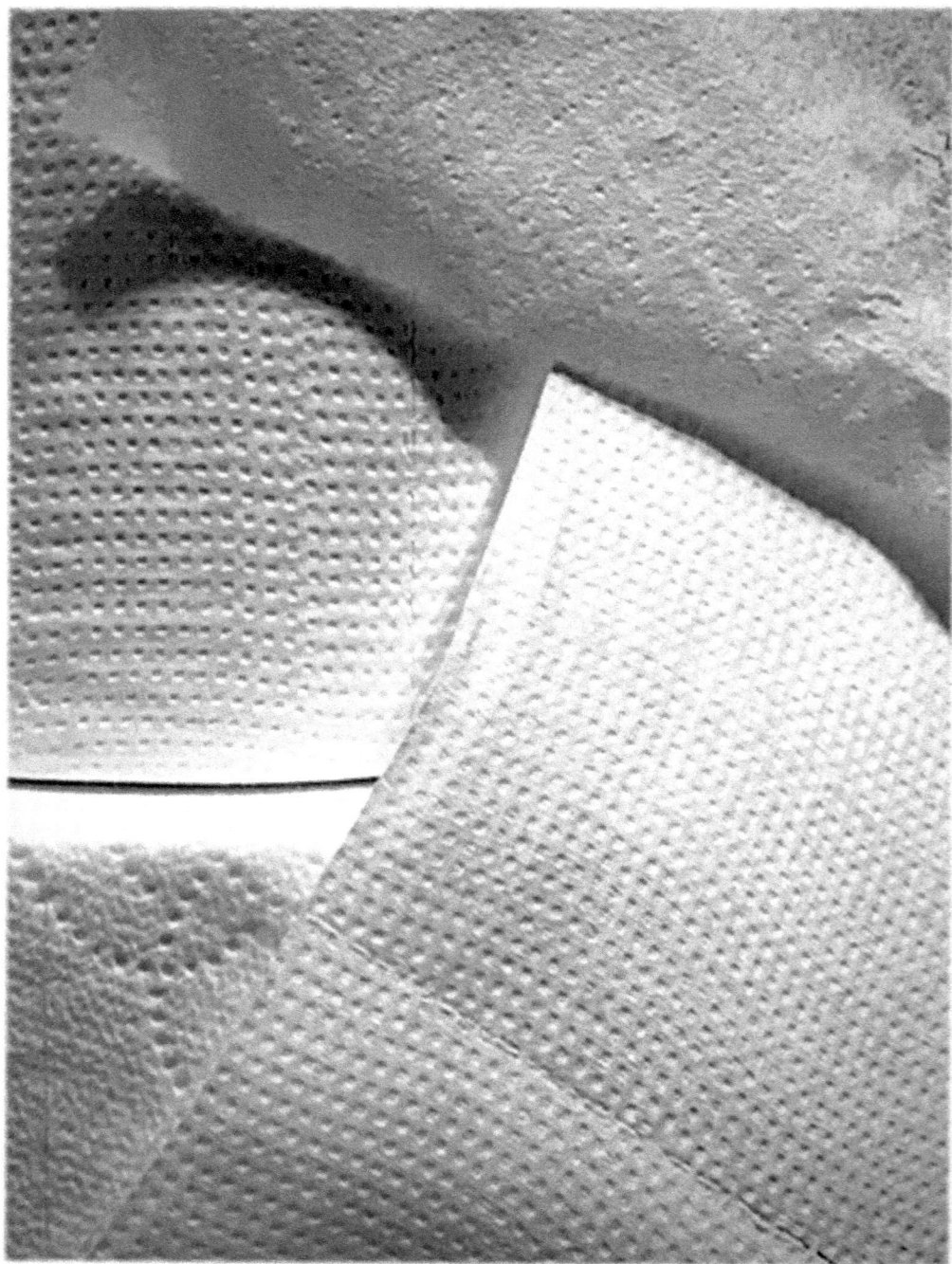

past or future

strategic or spontaneous

read the directions or fuck it up

why or why not

work it out or walk away

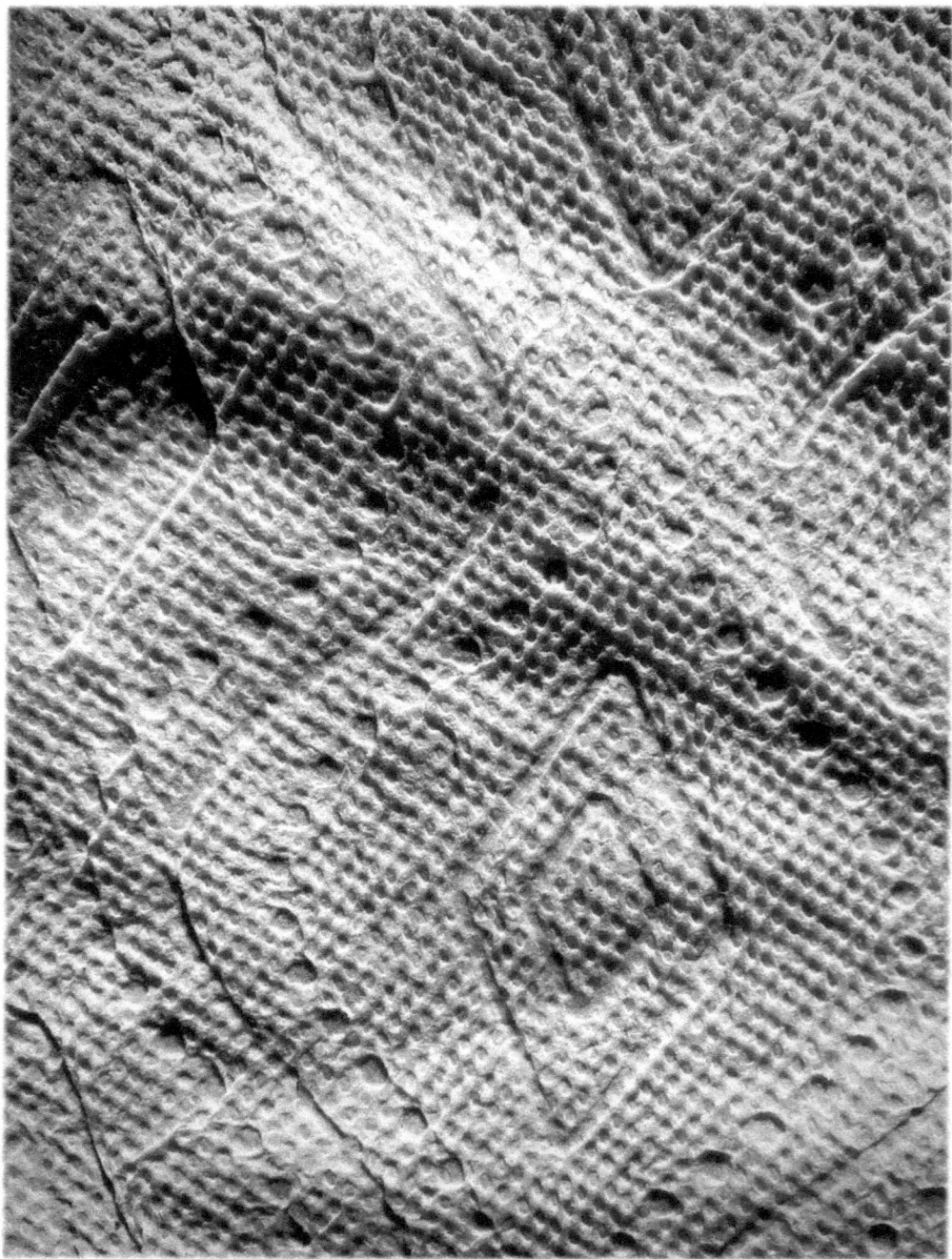

rock 'n roll or country

linkedin or facebook

2-step or foxtrot

tennis or football

kimmel or colbert

save or spend

cash or card

live to work or work to live

stocks or real estate

who pays?

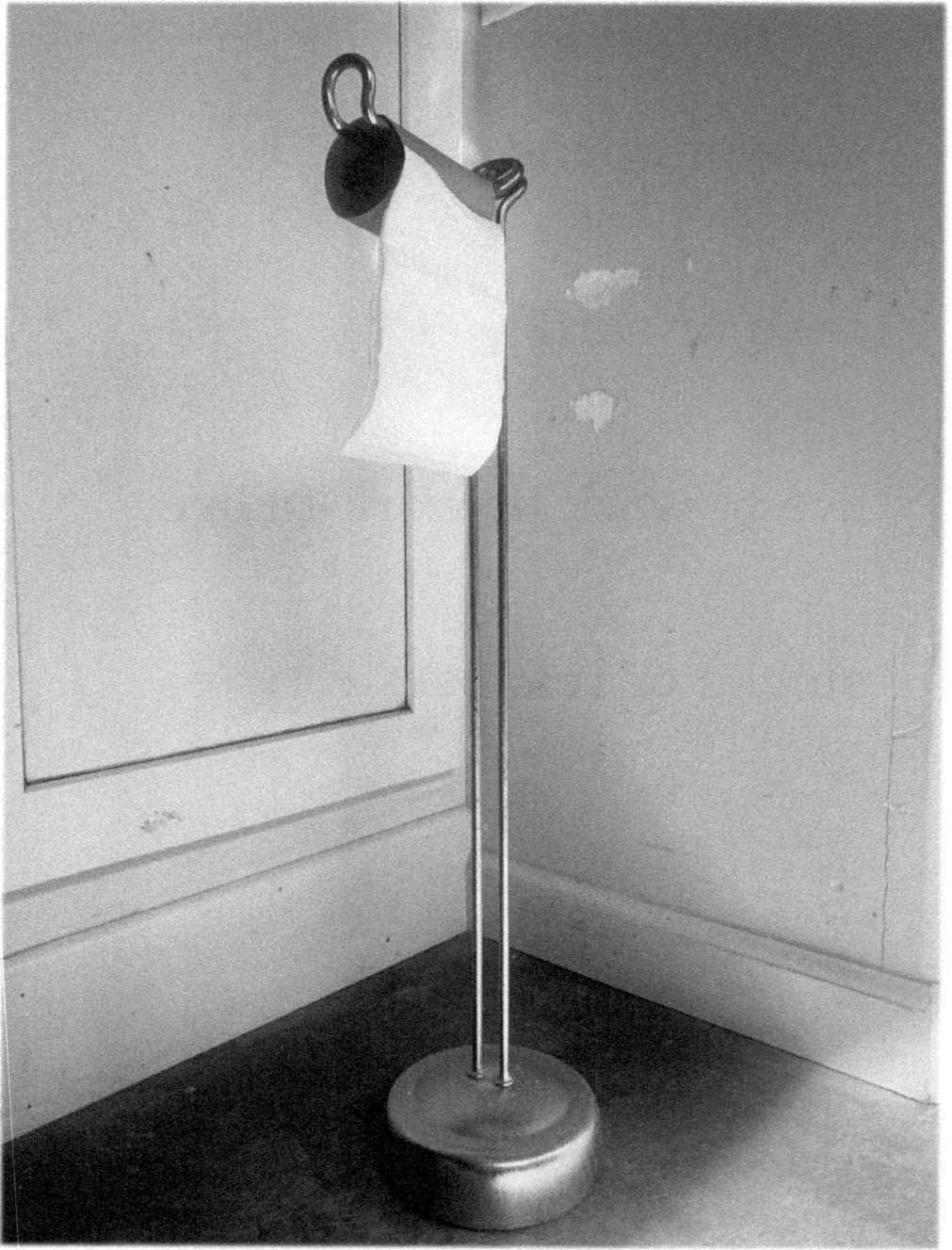

pet peeves

tell the truth

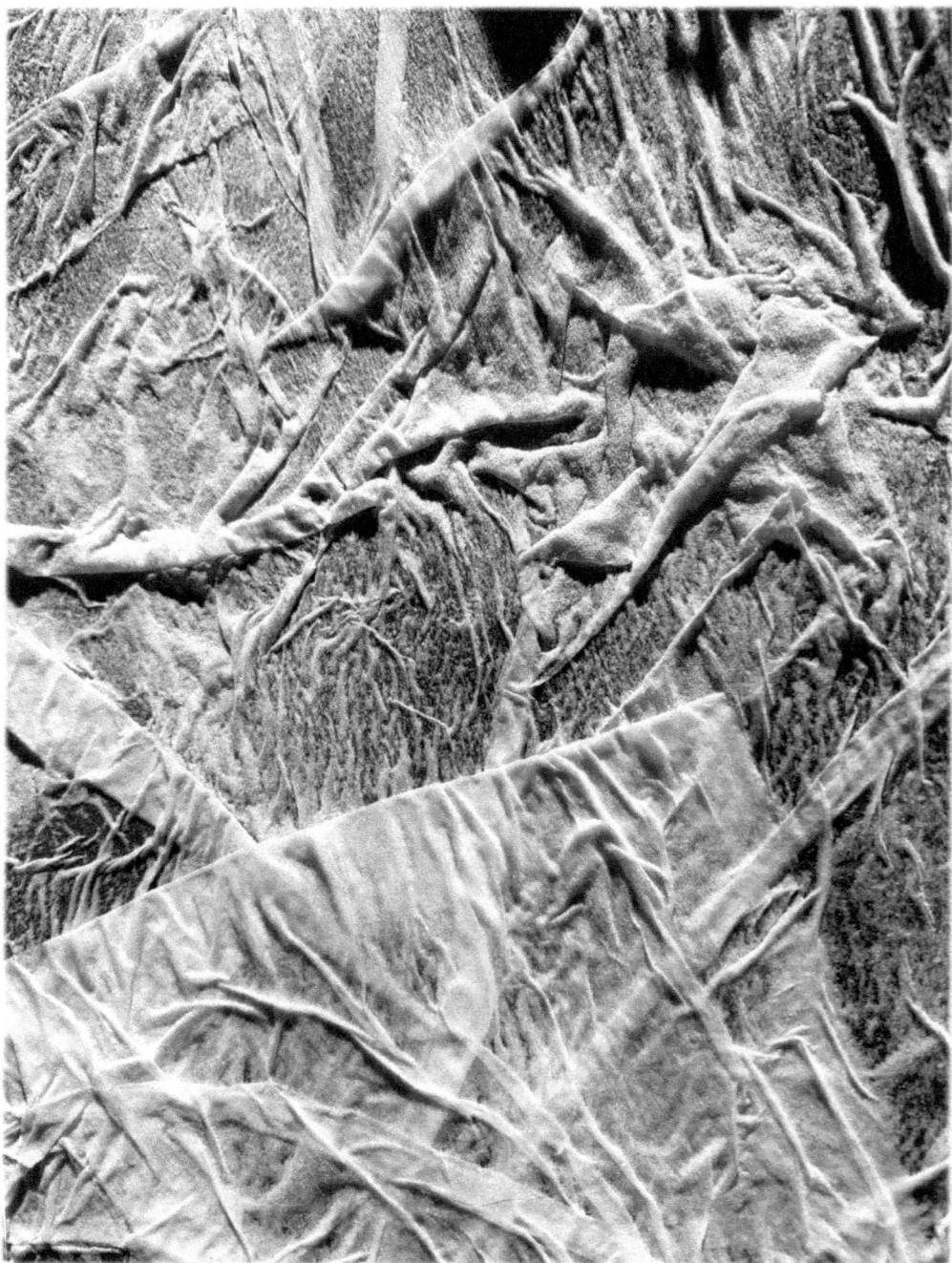

Level II

better...

cotton or silk

light or shadow

soap or shaving cream

sandalwood or chanel

washcloth?

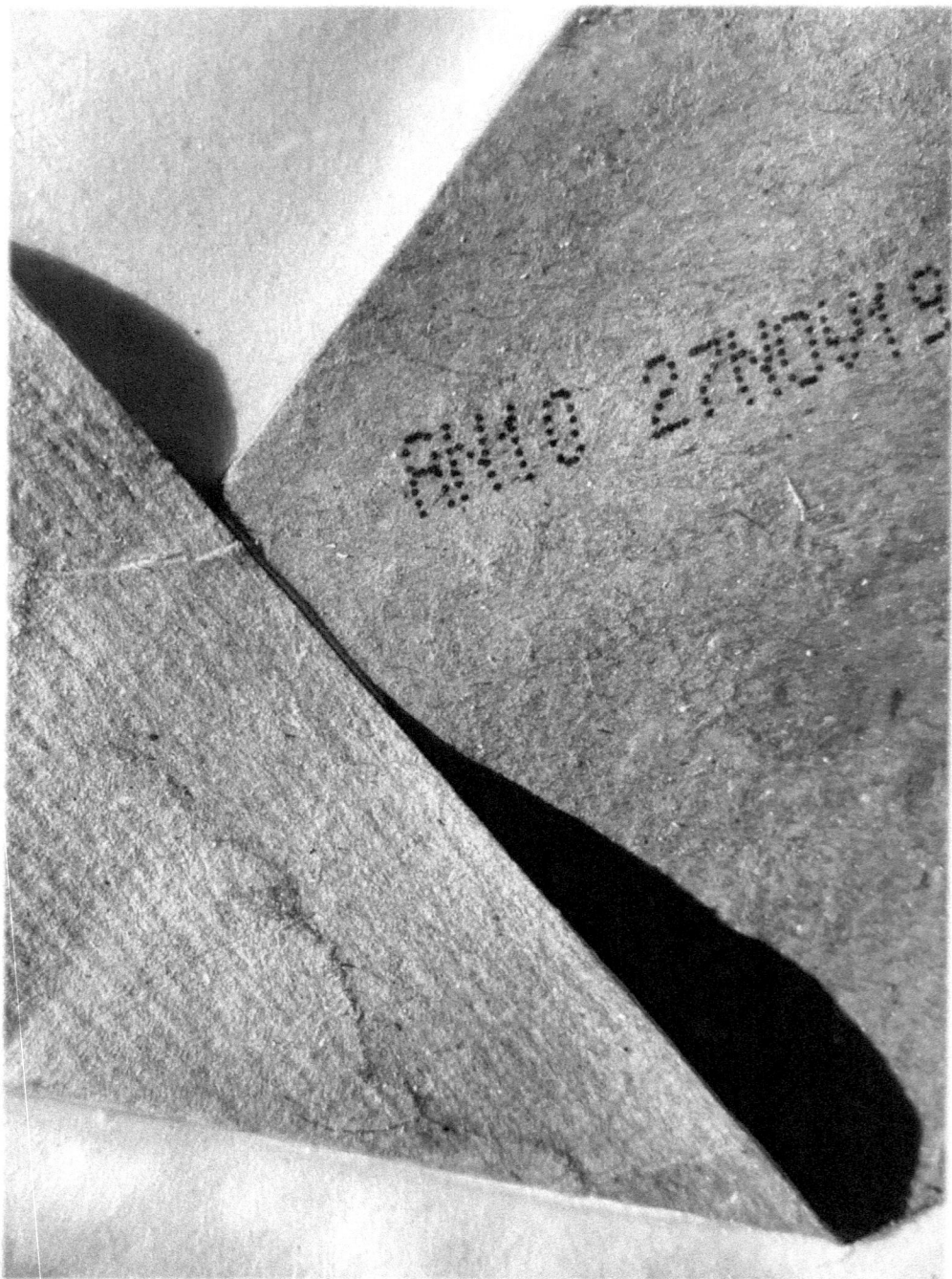

gold or silver

talk or text

fuss or fight

truth or consequences

make-up sex?

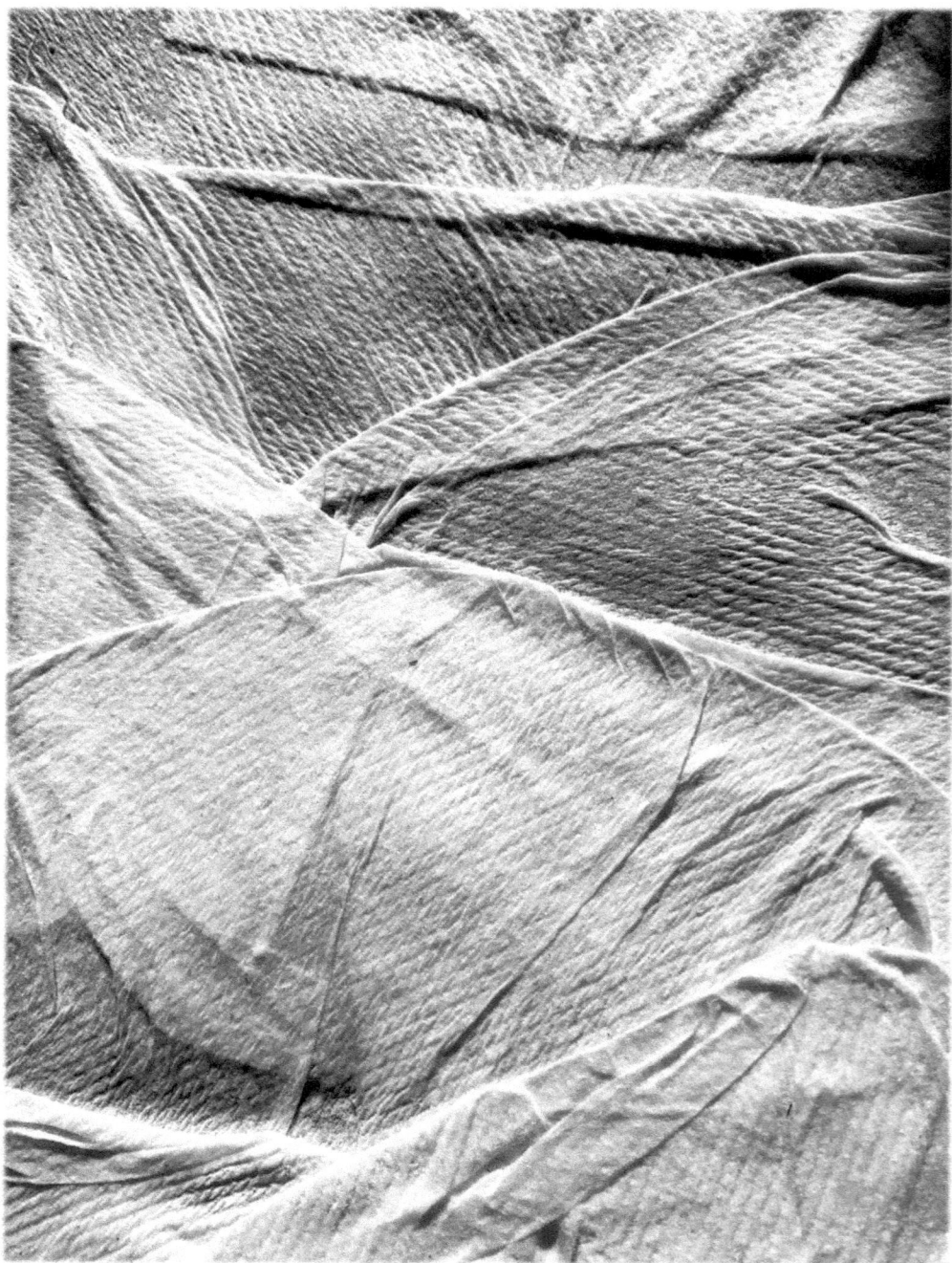

sassy or sincere

lipstick or chapstick

heels or bare feet

roses or daisies

bare or bush

safety or risk

trust or doubt

think or don't

happy or right

open up or shut down

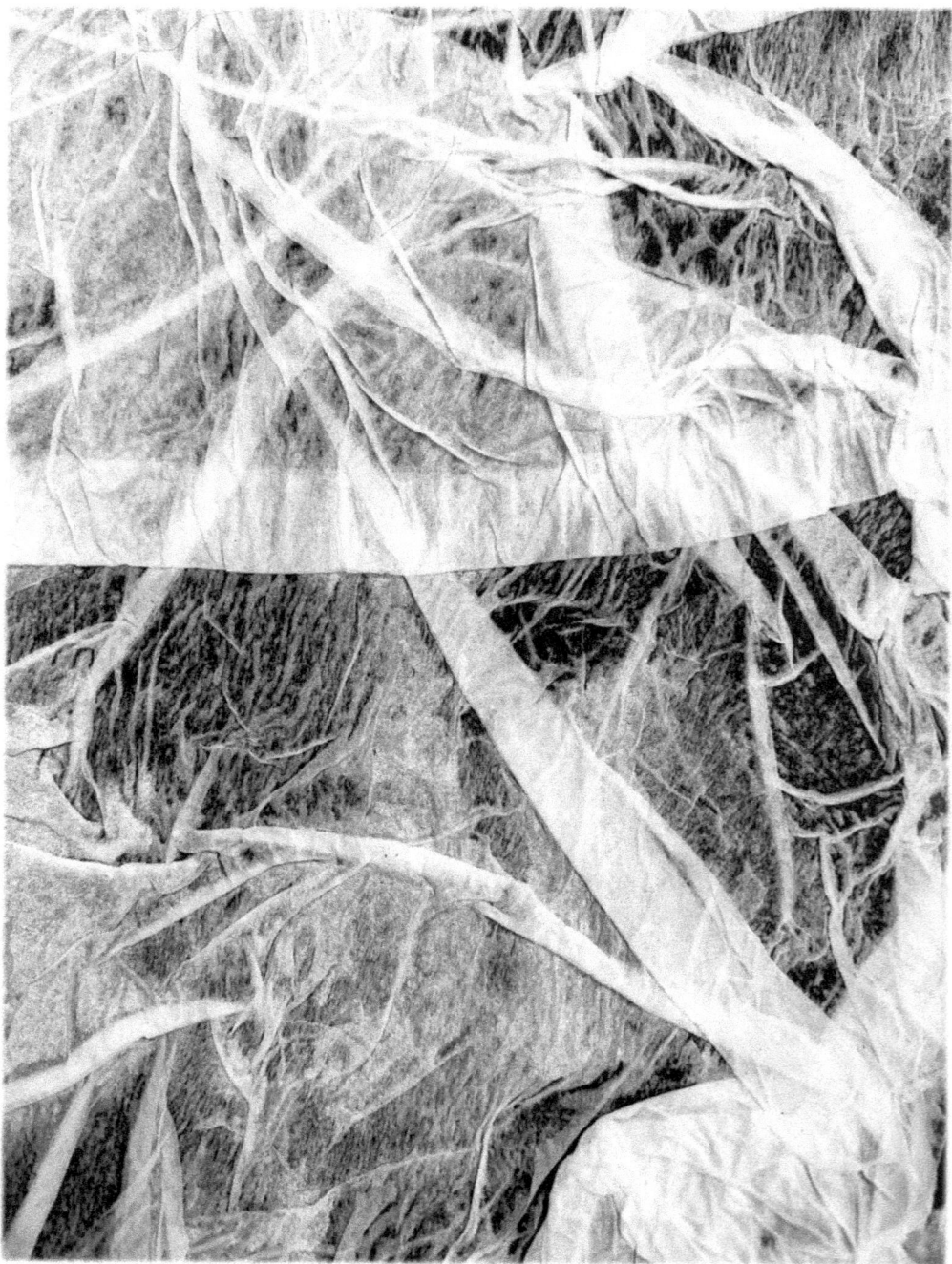

leather or lace

boxers or briefs

shower or bath

touch or tempt

hold it in or let it rip

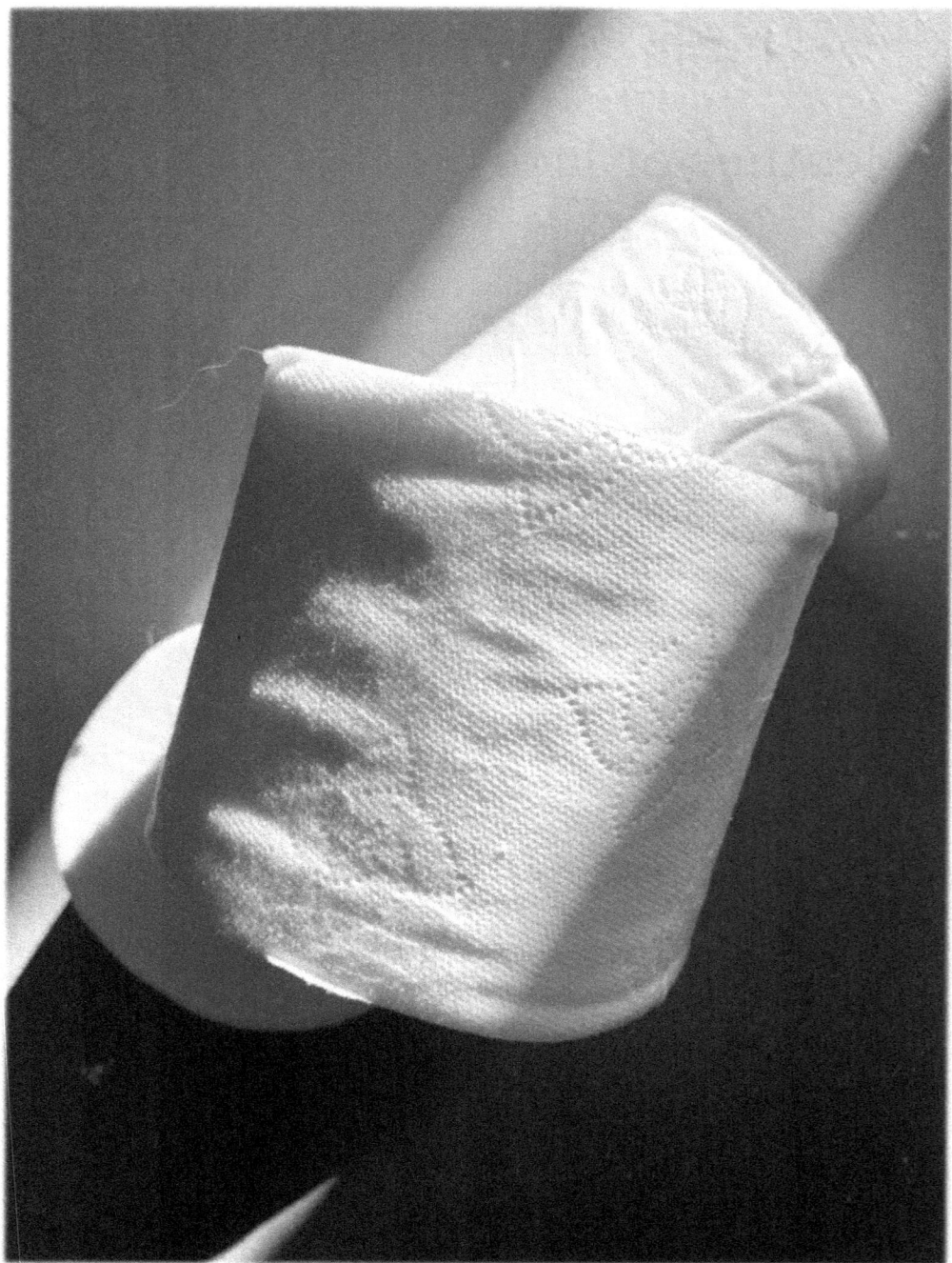

secrets

now, tell a secret.

take turns.

be brave.

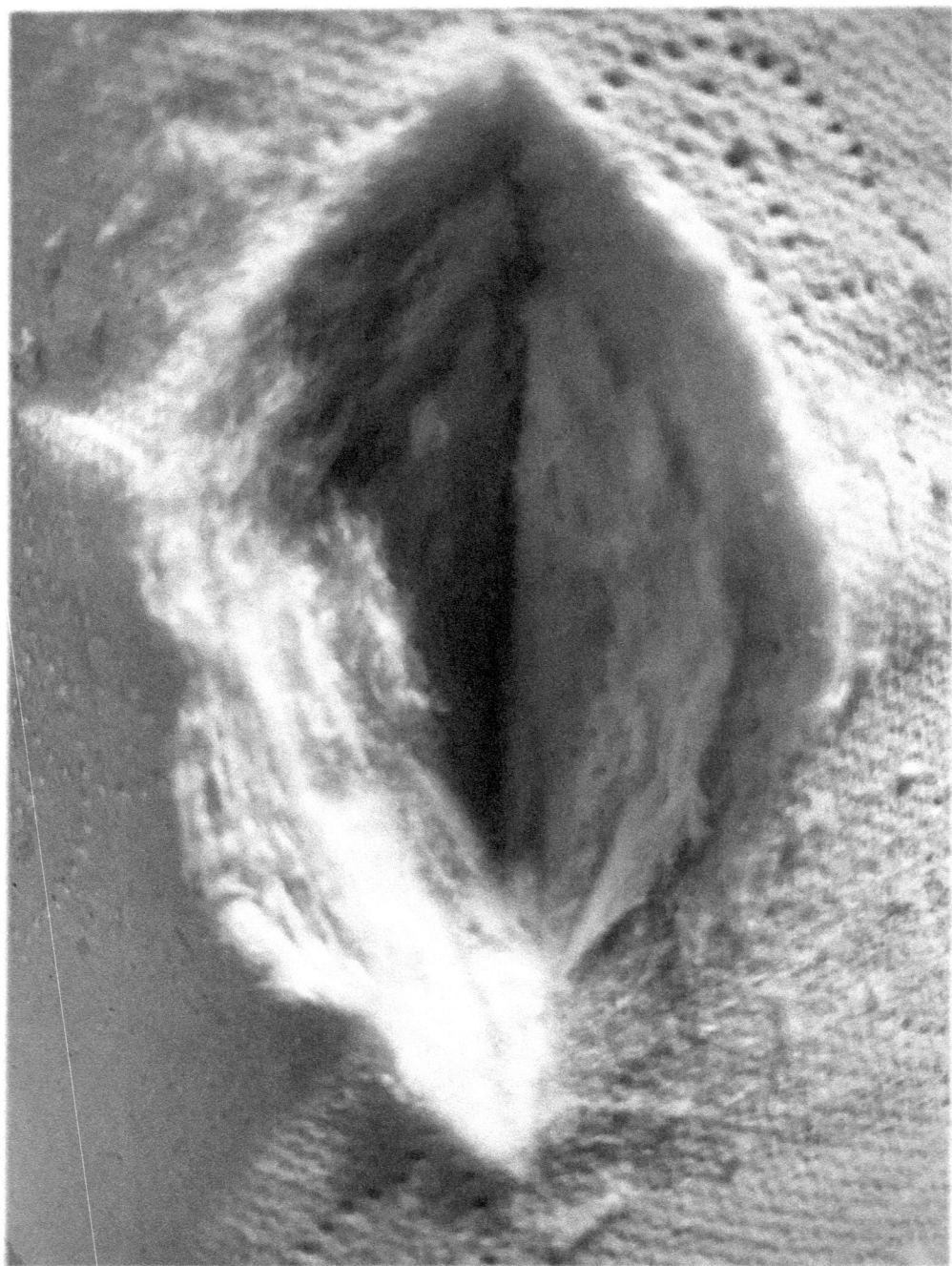

Level III

here's where it gets hard

bed

book or tv

firm or soft

talk or touch

room cool or warm

sheets?

left side or right

white noise or silence

pj's or nude

spoon or space

socks?

shower or bath

lights on or off

nibble or bite

tickle or stroke

finger or tongue

gentle or rough

top or bottom

slow or fast

eyes open or closed

kitchen counter?

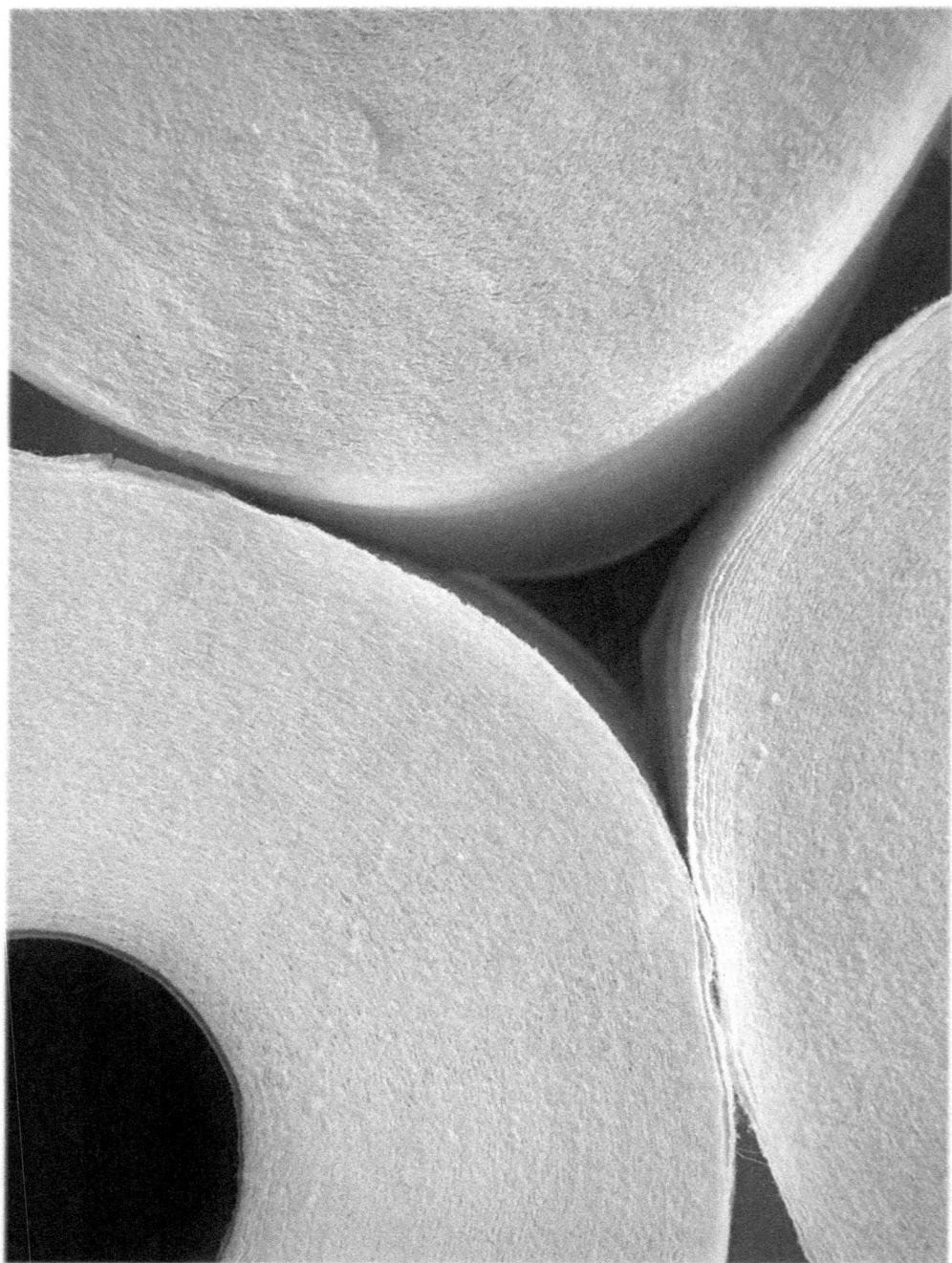

lick or suck

one finger or two

69 or taking turns

moan or scream

now or later

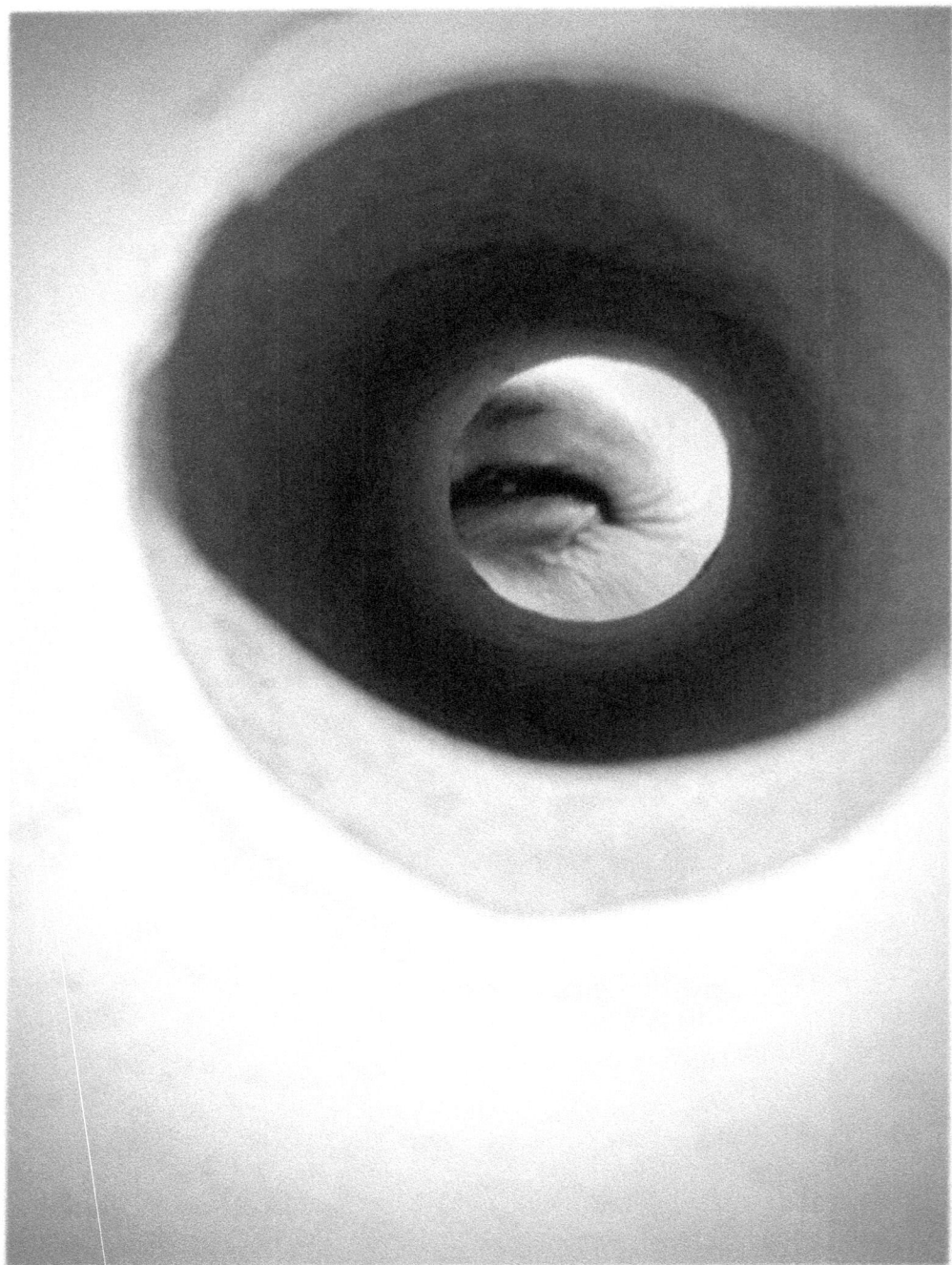

yes

please participate in volume II.

share your

feedback
comments
suggestions
ideas
& experiences.

email: info@beminequarantine.com

website: www.beminequarantine.com

thank you.

www.ingramcontent.com/pod-product-compliance
Lightning Source LLC
Chambersburg PA
CBHW032121280326
41933CB00009B/936